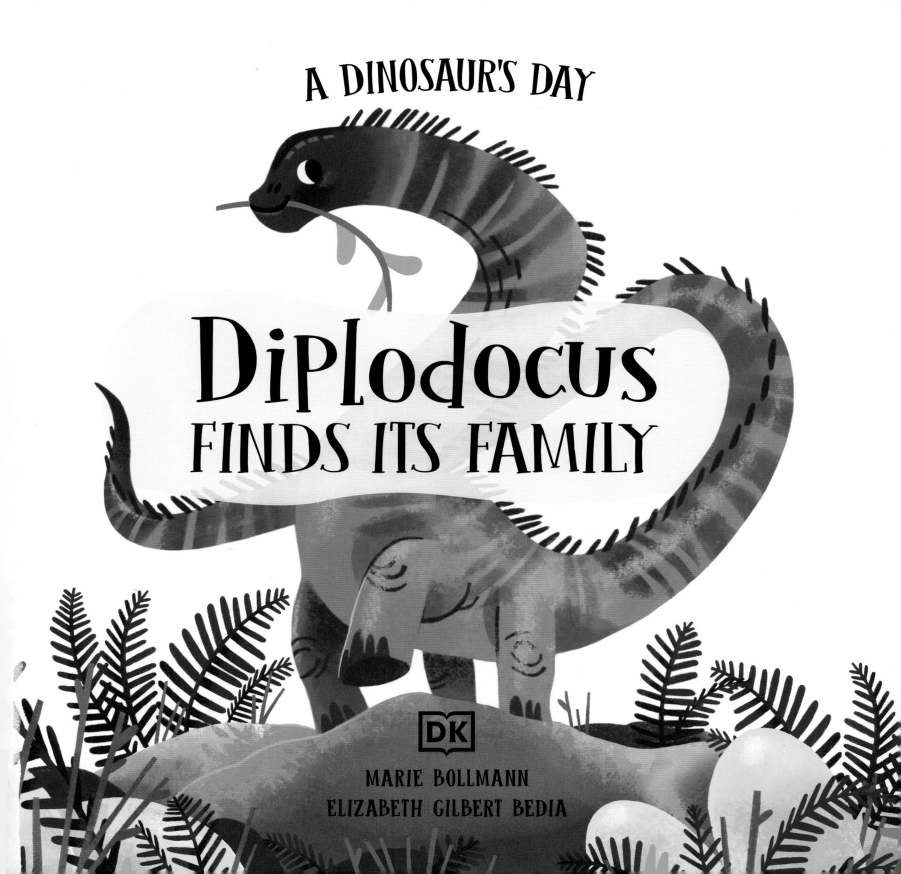

A DINOSAUR'S DAY

Diplodocus
FINDS ITS FAMILY

DK

Marie Bollmann
Elizabeth Gilbert Bedia

Sturdy. Shrewd. Spirited.
This is Diplodocus. Diplodocus means "double beam."

Come along on this sauropod's first day as
he learns to hide and seek in the Jurassic world.

Ready or not, here we come!

A tiny sound echoes through the morning mist.

It is coming from an egg the size of a bowling ball hidden in the forest underbrush.

What's beneath the shell?
The egg shifts and shakes, until...

CRACKKK!

Diplodocus! He blinks as the bright sunlight spills across the forest floor. He stretches his body, from his little head to his trunklike legs to his whip-like tail.

Suddenly...

CRACKKK!

Another egg hatches.

CRACKKK!

And another.

But where's Mom? The Diplodocus hatchlings stand up, ready to take on the world, until...

BOOM!

BOOM!

the ground begins to
rumble beneath them.

BOOM!

Smelling the damp air, **Allosaurus** slows.
Allosaurus has two powerful legs, a massive
body, razor-sharp teeth, and an enormous...

ROARRR!

The Diplodocus hatchlings SCATTER!
Allosaurus smells the makings of
a tasty morning snack.

SNIFF!

SNIFF!

SNIFF!

Little Diplodocus hides deep in the giant fern leaves to blend in. **Shrewd.**

Allosaurus comes closer and closer, but wait!

BOOM! BOOM!

Lucky for little Diplodocus, Allosaurus has found another dinosaur to chase— **Stegosaurus.**

Phew!

Where did the other hatchlings go?

Diplodocus stops to listen, but all he hears is...

Rumble.
Grumble.
Grumble.

Is it another dinosaur? No! It's his belly! He is a hungry herbivore, and this hiding place is very tasty!

MUNCH. CHOMP. GULP.

He snacks on juicy ferns, waxy
gingkoes, crunchy cycads—
even some pebbles!

MUNCH.
CHOMP.
GULP.

YUM!

Diplodocus is growing **fast**,
so he needs to eat **a lot!**

With a full belly, Diplodocus dozes off
under the giant fern. But his slumber
doesn't last long because...

someone is tickling his nose!

Flit. Flit. Flutter.

Flit. Flit. Flutter.

Libellulium has landed right on his nose.

A-choo!

Flit. Flit. Flutter.

Libellulium flutters away. **Spirited.**

Diplodocus bounds after it. Wait!

Maybe Libellulium knows
where Diplodocus's family is?

Libellulium flies on.

Diplodocus bounds along.

Weaving under the giant bellies
of one, two, three **Brachiosauruses**.

Oh my!

Libellulium tiptoes across the spiky
tail of a grazing Stegosaurus, and
Diplodocus follows.

Little Diplodocus zigzags through the fleet feet of **Dryosaurus**.

And he runs away from the
giant mouth and horned
nose of **Ceratosaurus.**

As Libellulium flies off across the river, little Diplodocus's first adventure-filled day draws to a close, and all he can think of is...

FOOD!

Munch. Chomp. Gulp.

One day, Diplodocus will **GROW** into one of the longest and largest dinosaurs to ever walk the Earth.

But for now, he just wants to be with what he has been searching for all day.

Family!

Who was Diplodocus?

Diplodocus was a herbivore, which meant it ate plants for food.

Diplodocus was a huge dinosaur with a long neck and tail.

Diplodocus had little spines running along its back.

Diplodocus was one of the largest animals ever. A fully grown diplodocus was about as long as a blue whale!

Diplodocus traveled in big groups, called herds, for safety.

Diplodocus lived about 150 million years ago in what is now North America.

Diplodocus could use its tail like a whip to defend itself.

How to say...

Diplodocus
di-PLO-doh-kus

Allosaurus
AL-oh-SORE-us

Stegosaurus
STEG-oh-SORE-us

Libellulium
li-BELL-ooh-lee-um

Brachiosaurus
brackee-oh-SORE-us

Dryosaurus
DRY-oh-SORE-us

Ceratosaurus
seh-RAT-oh-SORE-us

What do those words mean?

Carnivore
An animal that hunts and eats other animals.

Cycad
A type of plant common when dinosaurs lived.

Fern
A leafy plant that was eaten by lots of dinosaurs.

Ginkgo
One of the oldest types of trees.

Hatchling
A newly-hatched baby animal.

Herbivore
An animal that eats plants for food.

Jurassic
The second of the three time periods when dinosaurs lived.

Sauropod
A group of huge plant-eating dinosaurs.

About the illustrator

Marie Bollmann is a freelance illustrator who specializes in children's books. Marie was born in Münster, Germany, and is now based in Hamburg. She likes creating colorful, detailed illustrations, and her favorite dinosaur is Triceratops.

About the author

Elizabeth Gilbert Bedia is a former teacher and audiologist. She loves creating stories about our amazing world. She is the author of *Bess the Barn Stands Strong*, and *Balloons for Papa*. She lives in central Iowa with her dinosaur-loving family. You can visit her at www.elizabethgilbertbedia.com.

About the consultant

Dougal Dixon is a Scottish paleontologist, geologist, author, and educator. He has written more than 100 books, including the seminal work of speculative biology *After Man*, and award-winning *Where the Whales Walked*.

DK | Penguin Random House

Illustrator Marie Bollmann
Text for DK by Elizabeth Gilbert Bedia & Et Al Creative
Acquisitions Editors Fay Evans, James Mitchem
US Senior Editor Shannon Beatty
Project Art Editor Charlotte Bull
Consultant Dougal Dixon
Publishing Coordinator Issy Walsh
Senior Production Editor Nikoleta Parasaki
Senior Production Controller Inderjit Bhullar
Deputy Art Director Mabel Chan
Publishing Director Sarah Larter

First American Edition, 2022
Published in the United States by DK Publishing
1450 Broadway, Suite 801, New York, NY 10018

Illustrations copyright © Marie Bollmann 2022
Copyright in the layouts and design
of the work will vest in the publisher.
© 2022 Dorling Kindersley Limited
DK, a Division of Penguin Random House LLC
22 23 24 25 26 10 9 8 7 6 5 4 3 2 1
001-327011-Sep/2022

A catalog record for this book
is available from the Library of Congress.
ISBN 978-0-7440-5654-9

DK books are available at special discounts when purchased in bulk for sales promotions, premiums, fund-raising, or educational use. For details, contact: DK Publishing Special Markets, 1450 Broadway, Suite 801, New York, NY 10018 SpecialSales@dk.com

Printed and bound in China

For the curious
www.dk.com

This book was made with Forest Stewardship Council™ certified paper – one small step in DK's commitment to a sustainable future. For more information go to www.dk.com/our-green-pledge

FSC
www.fsc.org
MIX
Paper | Supporting responsible forestry
FSC™ C018179